todd huis[ken]

More mormon ORIGAMI

todd huisken

More mormon ORIGAMI

CFI
An Imprint of Cedar Fort, Inc.
SPRINGVILLE, UTAH

ISBN 978-1-4621-1509-9

Published by CFI, an imprint of Cedar Fort, Inc.
2373 W. 700 S., Springville, UT 84663
Distributed by Cedar Fort, Inc., www.cedarfort.com

Library of Congress Control Number: 2014945652

Cover and interior layout design by Shawnda T. Craig
Cover design © 2014 Lyle Mortimer
Edited by Jessica B. Ellingson

Printed in Canada

10 9 8 7 6 5 4 3 2 1

Thanks to my talented & beautiful wife, Jill, & to my four remarkable kids: Kylie, Jolie, Sophie & Dean, who are the source of inspiration for all that I do.

Thank you to Andrew Hudson for his creativity & ingenuity in these complex designs & to Nick Robinson for his artistic illustrations.

CONTENTS

INTRODUCTION
to origami

Origami (pronounced or-i-GA-me) is a Japanese word that means "to fold paper" & is known as the Japanese art of folding paper into shapes representing objects. Paper folding has been practiced for thousands of years. first beginning between AD 100-200 in China. But even though origami began in China. it didn't become widely popular until the Japanese took a liking to it in AD 600.

In the beginning. when paper was first invented & was expensive. origami was used for religious ocassions such as weddings & Chinese tea ceremonies. But today. origami can be found in all types of settings. such as schools. churches. art galleries & museums. If you watch carefully. you can even spot origami figures on television.

You'll notice that each origami design in this book has a skill level listed at the top of the page. Skill level 1 is the easiest. so start there & then work your way up to the skill level 3 designs. which are the most challenging. An index at the back of the book will help you find designs based on skill level.

I hope you enjoy folding the designs in this book. which come from stories in the Book of Mormon. LDS Church history & modern-day temples.

ORIGAMI
TERMINOLOGY, SYMBOLS & FOLDS

FOLDS

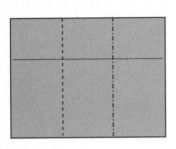 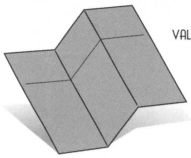

VALLEY FOLDS are represented by a dashed line:
MOUNTAIN FOLDS by a dot-dash line.
PRECREASES are shown with a thin line
that does not touch the sides:
all FOLDED or RAW EDGES are
shown with a thick line.

A RABBIT-EAR is a procedure where
four folds are made at once, meeting
at a vertex. Generally, you will
precrease all three of them,
and flatten the fourth into place.

 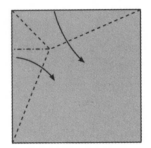 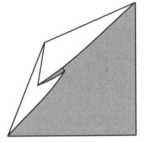

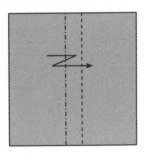 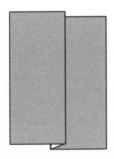

A PLEAT creates two creases,
one mountain & one valley.
Usually the mountain is
precreased & the valley is
flattened into place.

4

FOLDS

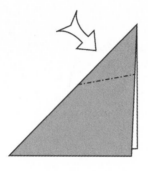 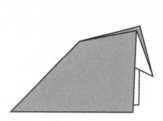

INSIDE REVERSE FOLDS change the direction of the spine of a flap, adding two creases along the way.

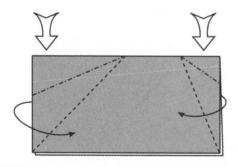 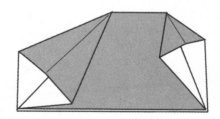

SQUASH FOLDS take the spine of a flap, open it up & flatten it. Usually the valley crease is precreased.

FOLDS

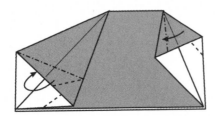 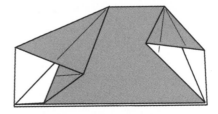

A SWIVEL fold takes an area of paper & pivots it around a vertex.
Swivel folds fall into the same group of operations as squash & reverse folds.

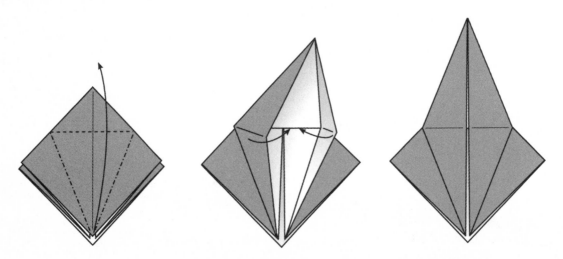

A PETAL fold is like doing two squash folds at once.
This is difficult. so try to precrease as much of it as possible first.

BOOK OF MORMON
DESIGNS

GREAT
& Spacious Building

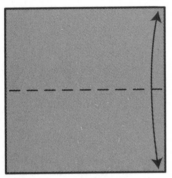

1. Start with a square piece of paper. Fold in half & unfold.

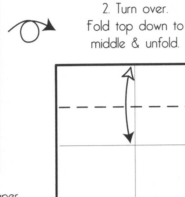

2. Turn over. Fold top down to middle & unfold.

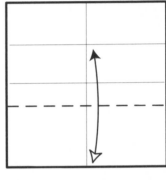

3. Fold bottom up to crease from step 2 & unfold.

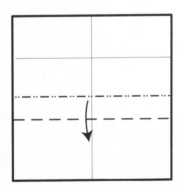

4. Pleat top half down over bottom half.

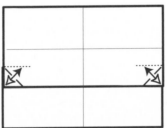

5. Fold & unfold corners where shown.

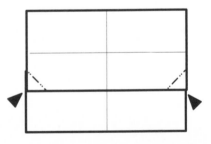

6. Open the paper slightly & push the corners inside (inside fold).

GREAT
& Spacious Building

7. Fold left & right sides toward middle.

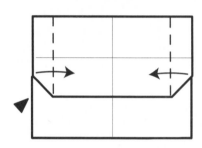

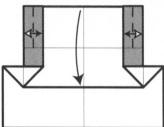

8. Fold sides in half & unfold.

9. Fold top down.

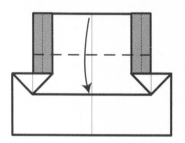

10. Fold top layer up.

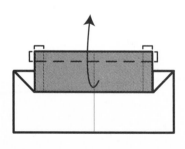

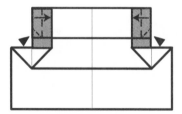

11. Fold sides in & fold flaps flat
(squash fold).

12. Match the width of the top
of the model with the fold in
the next step.

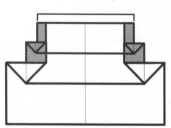

DID YOU KNOW:
According to Nephi. the great and spacious building was filled with people. They were mocking and pointing their fingers toward those who were partaking of the fruit.

GREAT
& Spacious Building

14. Slide the model from step 13 into the top of the first model.

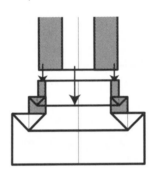

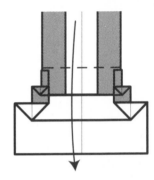

15. Fold top down.

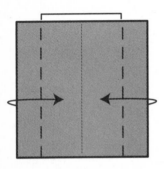

13. Using a second piece of square paper. fold sides in until width matches the width of the tower in step 12.

17. Fold sides in & fold flaps flat (squash fold).

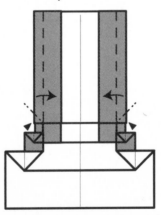

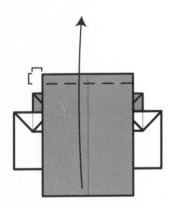

16. Fold top layer up.

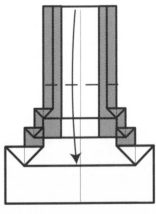

18. Fold top down.

GREAT
& Spacious Building

skill level: 2

DID YOU KNOW:
Limestone was the most common building material used in ancient America in Lehi's time.

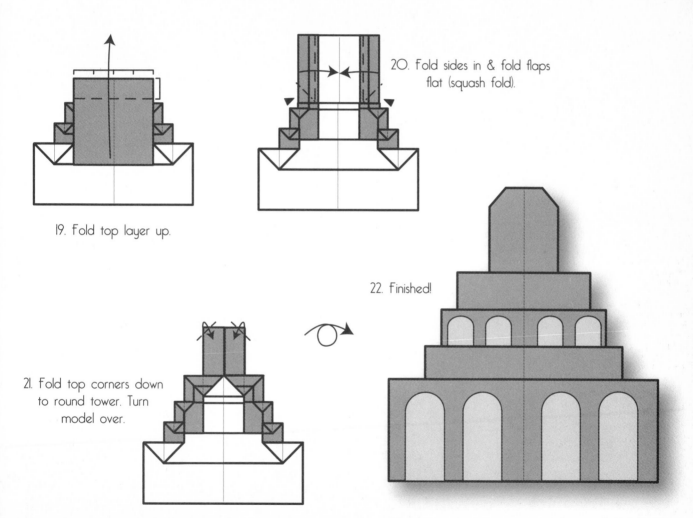

19. Fold top layer up.

20. Fold sides in & fold flaps flat (squash fold).

21. Fold top corners down to round tower. Turn model over.

22. Finished!

artwork: Nick Robinson

11

LAMANITE
Temple

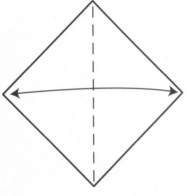

1. Start with a square piece of paper. Fold corner to corner & unfold.

2. Fold sides to center line.

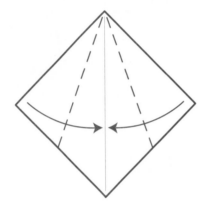

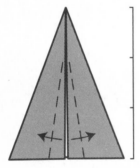

3. Fold bottom point back behind model.

4. Fold middle flaps out.

5. Pleat top down toward back.

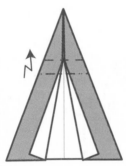

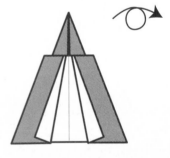

6. Turn paper over.

LAMANITE
Temple

QUIZ YOUSELF:
Where did wicked King Noah go to escape when he was being pursued by Gideon?

Mosiah 19:5

ANSWER:
He climbed to the top of the tower near the temple.

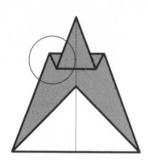

7. Corner to be folded. Fold & unfold the left flap.

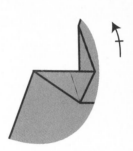

8. Fold side over & squash flap flat (squash fold).

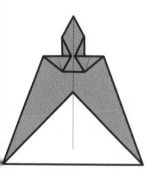

9. Repeat steps 7 & 8 with the other side. Turn paper over.

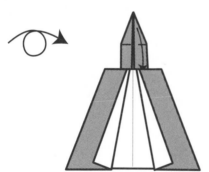

10. Fold top point down & tuck in.

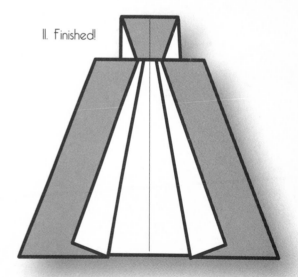

11. Finished!

artwork: Nick Robinson

13

NEPHITE
Temple

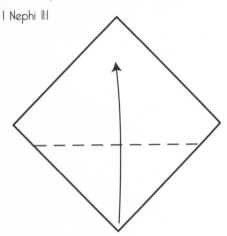

1. Start with a square piece of paper. Fold bottom corner toward top corner.

2. Turn paper over.

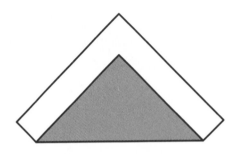

3. Fold sides toward center.

4. Turn paper over.

5. Fold bottom flaps up.

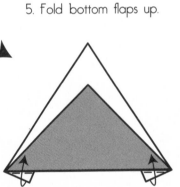

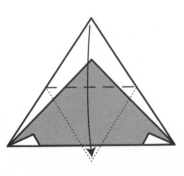

6. Fold top down behind bottom.

NEPHITE
Temple

DID YOU KNOW:
Temples in ancient America were traditionally rectangular & built with the east wall facing toward the sunrise & the north wall toward the North Star, Polaris.

7. Fold top layer up.

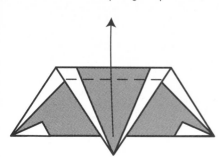

8. Corner to be folded.

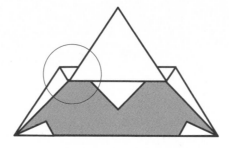

9. Fold & unfold left flap.

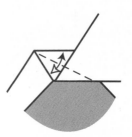

10. Fold left side in & squash flap flat (squash fold).

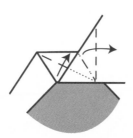

11. Repeat steps 8-10 on right side.

15

NEPHITE
Temple

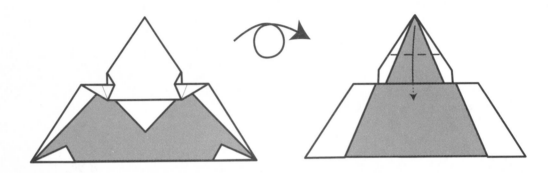

12. Turn model over.

13. Fold top down & tuck in.

14. Finished!

artwork: Nick Robins

ARMOR OF GOD
DESIGNS

NEPHITE
Helmet

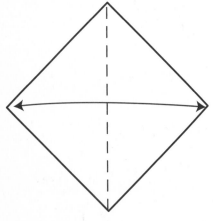

1. Start with a square piece of paper. Fold in half left to right & unfold.

2. Fold in half top to bottom.

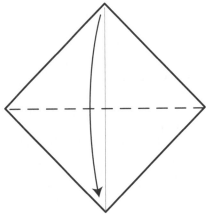

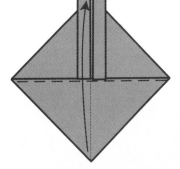

3. Fold top down.

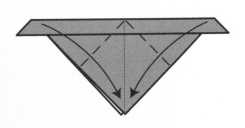

4. Fold right & left corners down.

5. Fold both sides of top layer up.

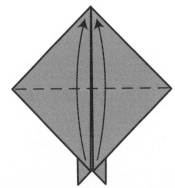

6. Fold middle layer up.

18

NEPHITE
Helmet

DID YOU KNOW:
Headgear among the ancient Americans was decorated with glyphs, feathers & cloth to show status & importance.

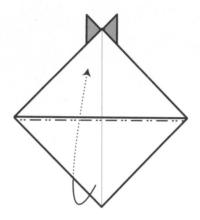

7. Fold bottom layer up & tuck inside.

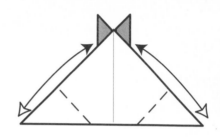

8. Fold & unfold bottom corners.

9. Open bottom of model & tuck corners inside.

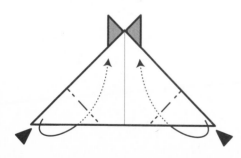

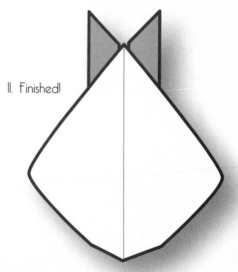

11. Finished!

10. Gently squeeze sides together to open helmet.

artwork: Nick Robinson

19

BREASTPLATE

QUIZ YOURSELF:
What two types of metal were the Jaredite breastplates made of?

Mosiah 8:10

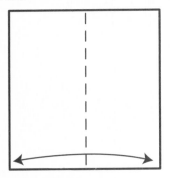

1. Start with a square piece of paper. Fold in half & unfold.

2. Fold left & right sides to middle.

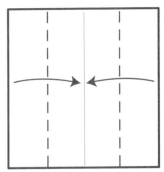

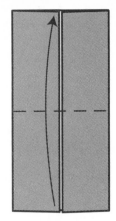

3. Fold bottom up.

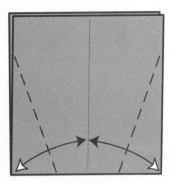

4. Fold bottom corners to the center line & unfold.

5. Open the paper slightly & push the bottom corners inside (inside fold).

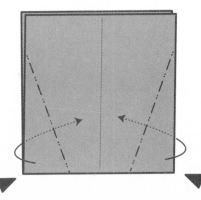

6. Fold top corners down & unfold.

BREASTPLATE

skill level: 1

DID YOU KNOW:
Most breastplates in Nephi's time were made of wood, bone, shells, jade & other stones, as well as various pieces of metal.

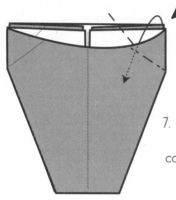

7. Open the paper slightly & push the top front corners inside (inside fold).

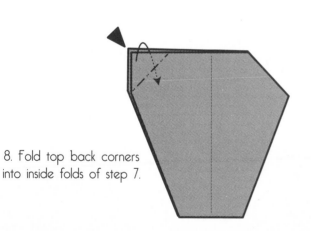

8. Fold top back corners into inside folds of step 7.

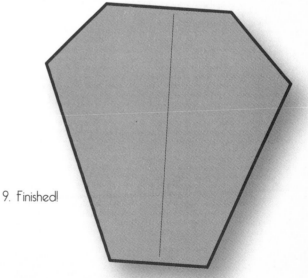

9. Finished!

artwork: Nick Robinson

21

QUIZ YOURSELF:
What was the name for suits of armor used by the Aztecs & their neighbors in which salt or some similar substance was placed between layers of cloth & the combination quilted loosely?

LOIN
Cloth

ANSWE
Ichcauipilli. This garment cou
withstand direct arrow impact. y
it was so light & cheap that t
Spaniards themselves adopted

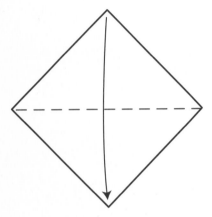

1. Start with a square piece of paper. Fold in half top to bottom.

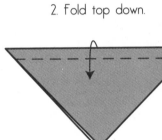

2. Fold top down.

3. Fold top down again.

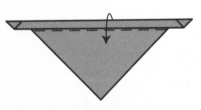

4. Fold top down a third time.

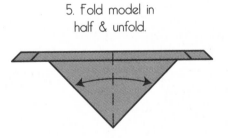

5. Fold model in half & unfold.

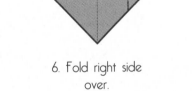

6. Fold right side over.

LOIN
Cloth

DID YOU KNOW:

There are eight distinct terms for armor mentioned in the Book of Mormon: breastplate (11 times). shields (10 times). armor (9 times). head-plates (7 times). arm-shields (2 times). animal skins (2 times). thick clothing (2 times) & bucklers (1 time).

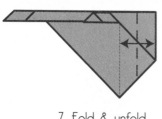

7. Fold & unfold right side.

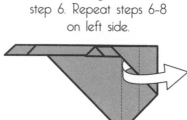

8 Unfold right side to step 6. Repeat steps 6-8 on left side.

9. Fold right side down.

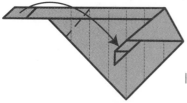

10. Fold left side down.

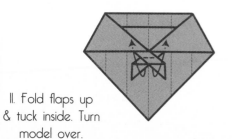

11. Fold flaps up & tuck inside. Turn model over.

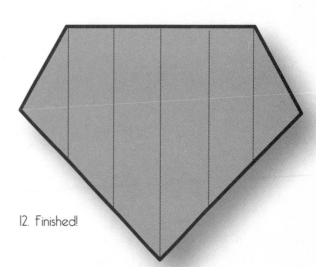

12. Finished!

artwork: Nick Robinson

BOOT

DID YOU KNOW:
Typically. shoes in Nephi's time were made of leather from goats. llamas. or sheep. or from plant fibers & were tied to the foot with leather or woven fabric straps.

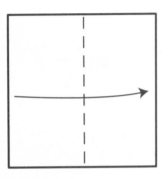

2. Fold in half again.

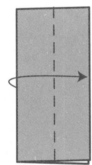

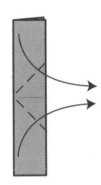

1. Start with a square piece of paper. Fold in half.

3. Fold top down & to the right. Fold bottom up & to the right.

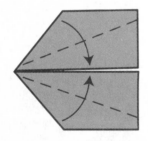

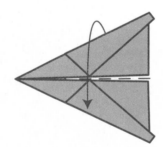

5. Fold in half.

4. Fold top down to middle. Fold bottom up to middle.

6. Fold front layer to the inside & up so it is between the top layer & bottom layer.

BOOT

skill level: 2

DID YOU KNOW:
The decoration of footwear in Nephi's time indicated a person's social status.

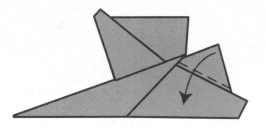

7. Fold flap down.

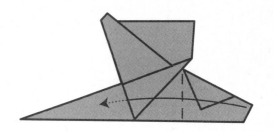

8. Fold right side over & tuck in.

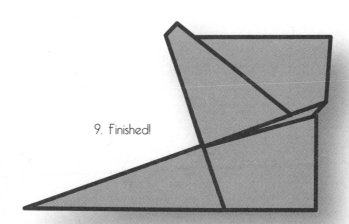

9. Finished!

artwork: Nick Robinson

SHIELD

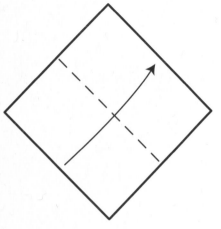

1. Start with a square piece of paper. Fold in half bottom to top.

2. Fold in half again bottom to top.

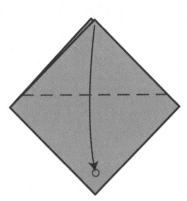

3. Fold top layer down.

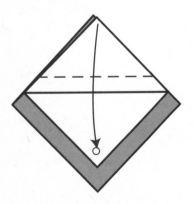

4. Fold second layer down.

5. Fold third layer down.

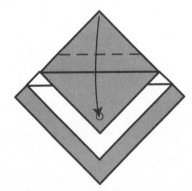

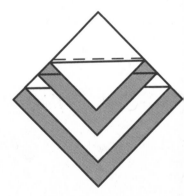

6. Turn paper over.

26

SHIELD

QUIZ YOURSELF:
What were the various parts of armor that Mormon wore before taking the title of liberty to the people?

Alma 46:13

ANSWER:
Head-plate, breastplate, shields & armor girded about his loins.

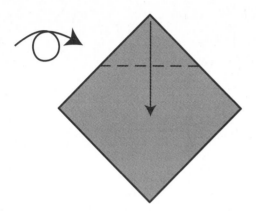

7. Fold top down.

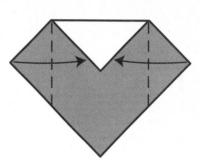

8. Fold left & right sides in.

9. Turn paper over.

10. Finished!

artwork: Nick Robinson

27

SWORD
of Laban

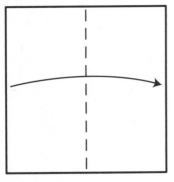

1. Start with a square piece of paper. Fold in half.

2. Fold in half again.

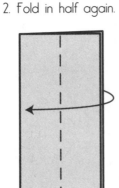

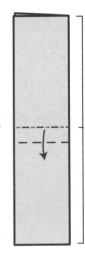

3. Using two folds, pleat the top half over the bottom.

4. Using two folds, pleat the bottom half over the top so the folded edges meet.

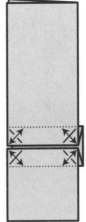

5. Fold & unfold the four corners of the top layer.

SWORD
of Laban

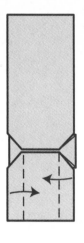

6. Fold the sides of bottom to middle. squash flaps flat (squash fold).

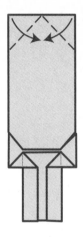

7. Fold top corners down to make a point.

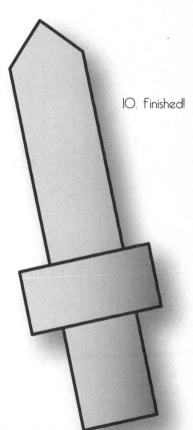

10. Finished!

8. Fold the sides of top to middle. squash flaps flat (squash fold).

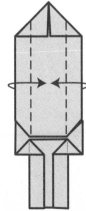

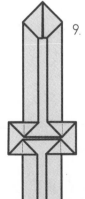

9. Turn paper over.

artwork: Nick Robinson

CHURCH HISTORY

—— DESIGNS ——

GOLD
Plates (NOTE: This model requires cutting)

ANSWER
Eleve

DID YOU KNOW:

At the beginning of the Book of Mormon, how many witnesses testify that they were shown the gold plates?

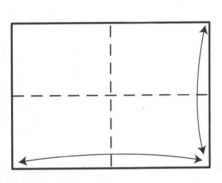

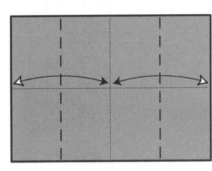

1. Start with a rectangular piece of paper. Fold in half & unfold. Fold in half the other way & unfold. Turn paper over.

2. Fold right & left sides to the middle & unfold.

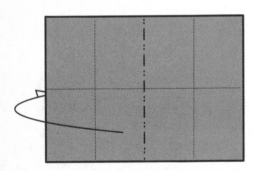

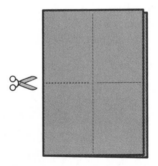

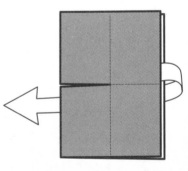

3. Fold left half behind.

4. Cut on crease halfway across from the left side.

5. Unfold the paper by bringing the bottom layer around to the left.

GOLD
Plates (NOTE: This model requires cutting)

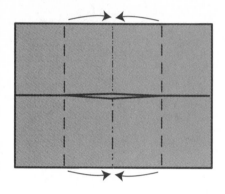

6. Push the right & left sides of the paper together so the middle pokes up.

7. Fold top & bottom sides down. The paper should look like an X.

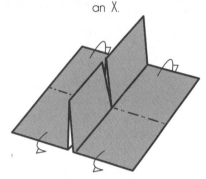

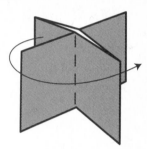

8. Fold the backside around to form the book.

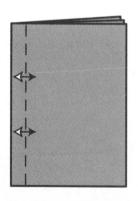

9. Fold & unfold the left side.

10. To form the rings. make six small cuts to the crease line where shown & either push the non-ring edges inside OR cut on dotted line where shown & remove the non-ring edges.

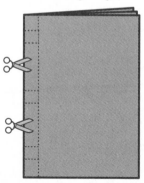

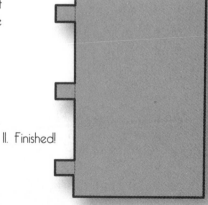

11. Finished!

artwork: Nick Robinson

33

DID YOU KNOW:
Wednesday is the day
new missionaries enter
into the MTC.

MISSIONARY
Badge (using square paper)

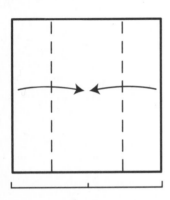

1. Start with a square piece of paper.
Fold left & right sides to middle.

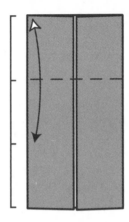

2. Fold top down where
shown & unfold.

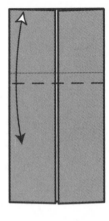

3. Fold top down slightly below
crease from step 2 & unfold.

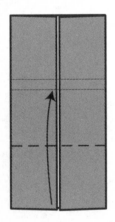

4. Fold bottom up to lower
crease from step 3.

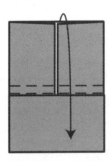

5. Fold top down at
crease from step 2.

6. Finished!

34

artwork: Nick Robin

MISSIONARY
Badge (using rectangle paper)

skill level: 1

DID YOU KNOW:
There are now 83,035 full-time missionaries in the world.

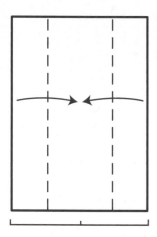

1. Start with a rectangular piece of paper. Fold left & right sides to middle.

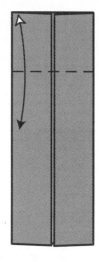

2. Fold top down where shown & unfold.

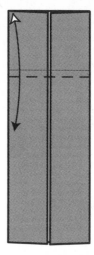

3. Fold top down slightly below crease from step 2 & unfold.

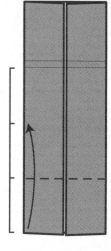

4. Fold bottom up where shown.

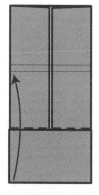

5. Fold bottom up again to lower crease from step 3.

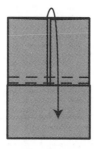

6. Fold top down at crease from step 2.

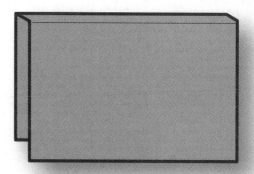

7. Finished!

artwork: Nick Robinson

SISTER
Missionary Outfit

DID YOU KNOW:
The first official proselyting sister missionaries for the LDS church were Inez Knight & Lucy Jane (Jennie) Brimhall. They were set apart in Provo, Utah, on April 1, 1898.

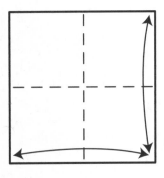

1. Start with a square piece of paper. Fold in half left to right & unfold. Fold in half top to bottom & unfold.

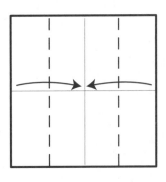

2. Fold right & left sides to middle.

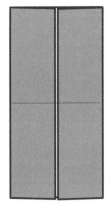

3. Turn paper over.

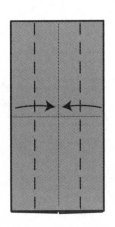

4. Fold left & right sides to middle.

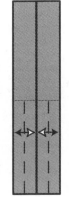

5. Fold left & right sides to middle on bottom half of model only & unfold.

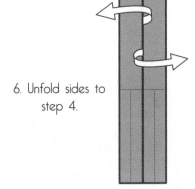

6. Unfold sides to step 4.

36

SISTER
Missionary Outfit

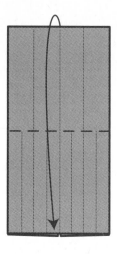

7. Fold in half top to bottom.

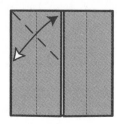

8. Fold corner to form crease & unfold.

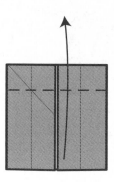

9. Fold top layer up where shown.

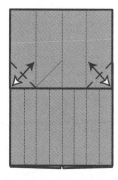

10. Fold left & right corners & unfold.

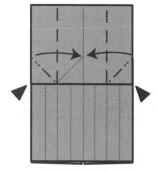

11. Fold top left & right sides to middle while pushing in corners & folding flaps flat (squash fold).

SISTER
Missionary Outfit

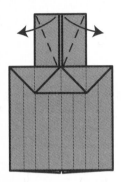

12. Fold top layers down.

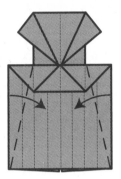

13. Fold bottom left & right sides in at an angle.

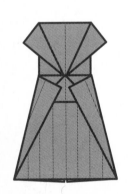

14. Turn model over.

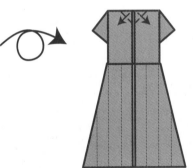

15. Fold down corners.

16. Finished!

artwork: Nick Robin

STATE
of Utah

DID YOU KNOW:
Spelled backward, the Utah city Levan is "navel." It is so named because it is in the middle of Utah.

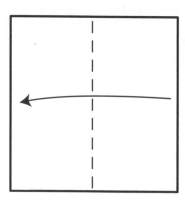

1. Start with a square piece of paper. Fold in half right to left.

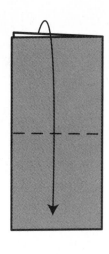

2. Fold in half top to bottom.

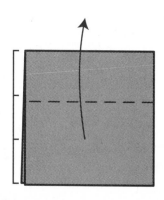

3. Fold top layer up where shown.

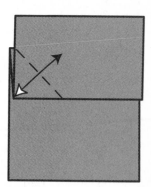

4. Fold left corner & unfold.

STATE
of Utah

QUIZ YOURSELF:
What is the official Utah State fish?

ANSWER
The rainbow trou

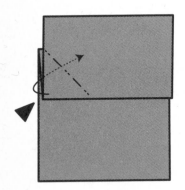

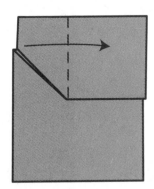

6. Fold left side over (completes squash fold).

5. Open slightly & push in corner (inside fold).

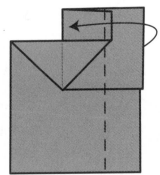

7. Fold right side over. Turn model over.

8. Finished!

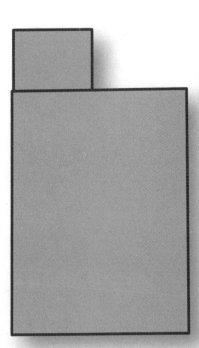

artwork: Nick Robins

BEEHIVE

DID YOU KNOW:
The beehive became the
official emblem for Utah
on March 4. 1959.

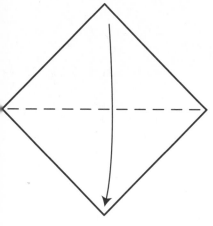

1. Start with a square piece
of paper. Fold in half top to
bottom.

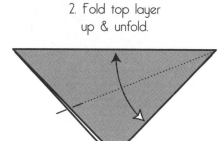

2. Fold top layer
up & unfold.

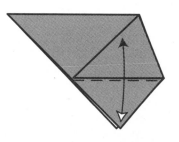

3. Fold right corner over.

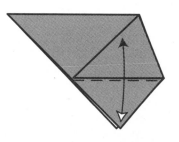

4. Fold both layers of
bottom up & unfold.

5. Fold top layer
up & tuck inside.

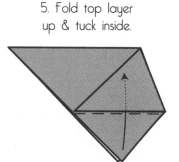

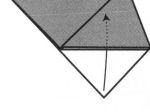

6. Fold bottom layer
up & tuck inside.

BEEHIVE

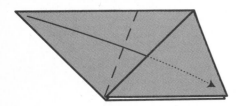

7. Fold left side over & tuck inside.

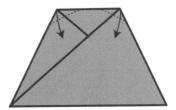

8. Fold down top corners to round top.

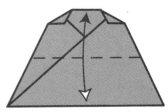

9. Fold in half & unfold.

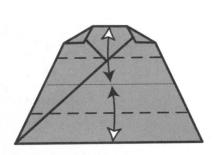

10. Fold bottom section in half & unfold. Fold top section in half & unfold. Turn paper over.

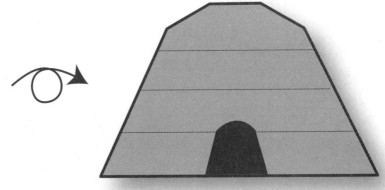

11. Finished!

artwork: Nick Robin

SEAGULL

QUIZ YOURSELF:
What year did the
California gull become
the Utah state bird?

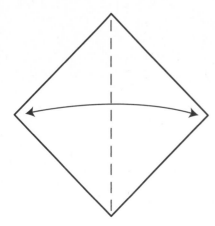

1. Start with a square piece of
paper. Fold in half side to side
& unfold.

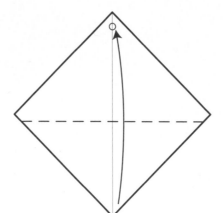

2. Fold bottom
corner up.

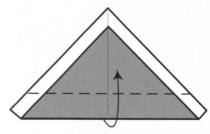

3. Fold bottom up.

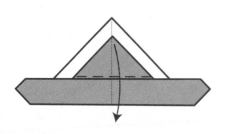

4. Fold top layer
down.

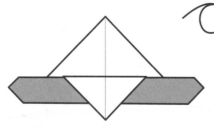

5. Turn paper over.

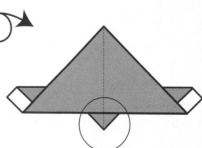

6. Pleat bottom
point up.

43

SEAGULL

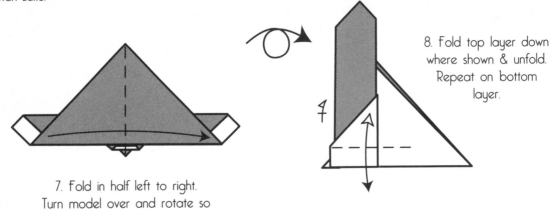

8. Fold top layer down where shown & unfold. Repeat on bottom layer.

7. Fold in half left to right. Turn model over and rotate so wings are pointed up

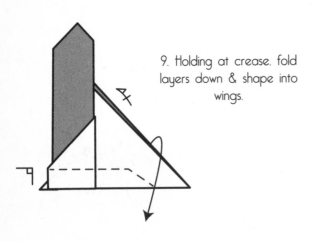

9. Holding at crease. fold layers down & shape into wings.

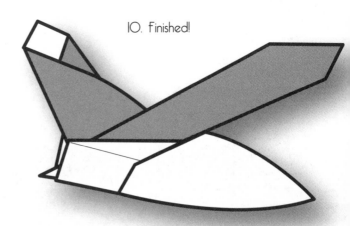

10. Finished!

artwork: Nick Robins

44

SALT LAKE
Tabernacle

DID YOU KNOW:
The Tabernacle was constructed completely by hand, with all materials hand-fashioned.

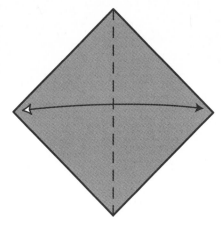

1. Start with a square piece of paper. Fold in half & unfold.

2. Fold sides to the center.

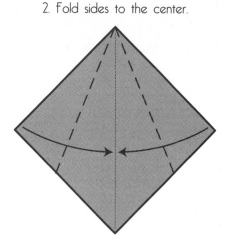

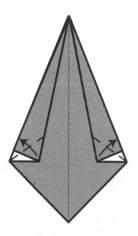

3. Fold flaps back out.

4. Fold corners of flaps up.

5. Fold bottom up & unfold. Turn paper over.

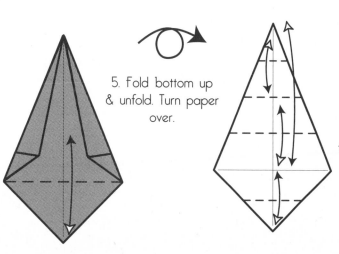

6. Fold the bottom in half to the crease & unfold. Fold the top in half to the crease twice & unfold so there are four sections. Turn model over.

45

SALT LAKE
Tabernacle

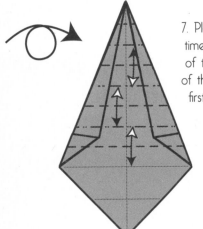

7. Pleat the top forward three times with the bottom crease of the top & the top crease of the bottom meeting on the first fold. Fold the top point down in a half pleat.

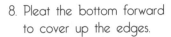

8. Pleat the bottom forward to cover up the edges.

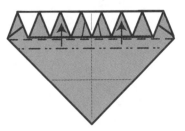

9. Turn paper over & rotate so the point is facing up.

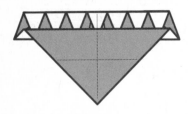

10. Fold top flap down on existing crease.

11. Fold the corners in to lock step 8 into place.

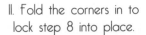

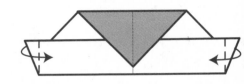

SALT LAKE
Tabernacle

QUIZ YOURSELF:
How was the pipe organ
in the Tabernacle originally
powered before electricity?

ANSWER:
City Creek ran through
Temple Square north of the
Tabernacle & was harnessed
with a water wheel to power
the huge organ inside.

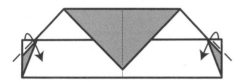

12. Fold corners in to
secure the lock in step 11.

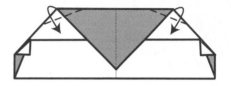

13. Fold the top corners
to round the roof.

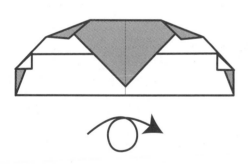

14. Turn paper over.

15. Finished!

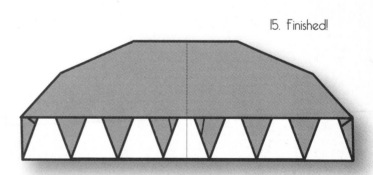

artwork: Nick Robinson

design: Andrew Hudson

47

LATTER-DAY TEMPLE

— DESIGNS —

BOUNTIFUL
Utah Temple

DID YOU KNOW:
Announcement: 2 February 1990.
Groundbreaking & Site
Dedication: 2 May 1992 by Ezra
Taft Benson.

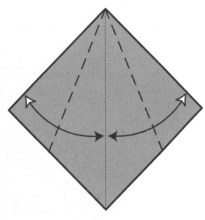

1. Start with a square piece of paper. Fold side corners down to center.

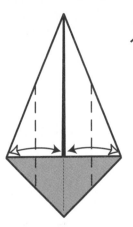

2. Fold side corners to center & unfold. Turn paper over.

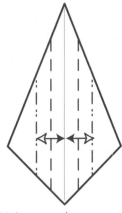

3. Make one pleat to center on each side & unfold. Turn paper over.

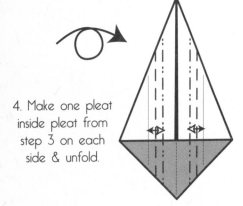

4. Make one pleat inside pleat from step 3 on each side & unfold.

5. Fold top behind.

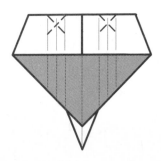

6. Fold & unfold four small creases to look like Xs where shown.

BOUNTIFUL
Utah Temple

DID YOU KNOW:
Public Open House: 4
November-17 December 1994.
Dedication: 8-14 January 1995
by Howard W. Hunter.

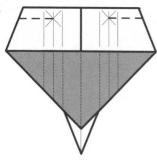

7. Fold & unfold to create two small creases where shown.

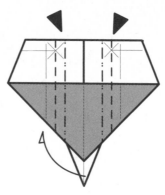

8. Begin folding back layer up & push in where shown.

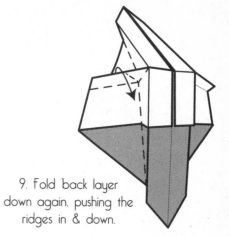

9. Fold back layer down again, pushing the ridges in & down.

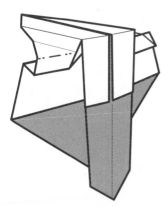

10. Steps 8-10 in progress. Fold back layer down so the model lies flat.

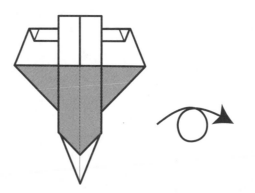

11. Turn paper over.

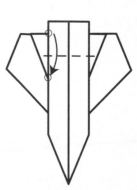

12. Fold point up.

BOUNTIFUL
Utah Temple

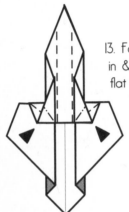

13. Fold both sides in & squash flaps flat (squash fold).

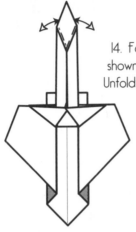

14. Fold where shown & unfold. Unfold to step 13.

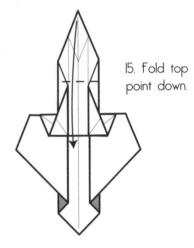

15. Fold top point down.

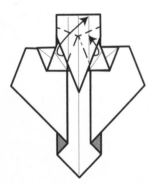

16. Fold point up using a rabbit-ear fold & creases from step 14. Then squash the other folds flat.

17. Fold sides to center to create a thin steeple.

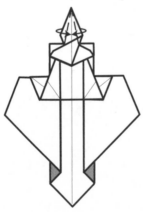

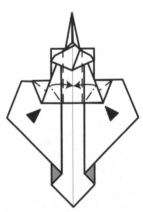

18. Fold sides in & squash flaps flat (squash fold).

BOUNTIFUL
Utah Temple

QUIZ YOURSELF:
he floor plan created for
e Bountiful Utah Temple
as adapted & used in
hat other Utah temple?

ANSWER:
The Mount Timpanogos
Utah Temple.

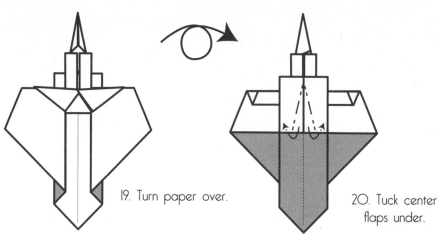

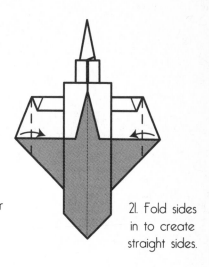

19. Turn paper over.

20. Tuck center flaps under.

21. Fold sides in to create straight sides.

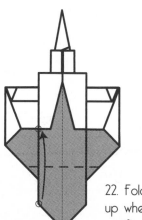

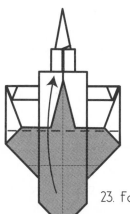

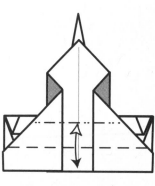

22. Fold bottom up where shown & unfold.

23. Fold bottom up.

24. Fold bottom up & unfold.

QUIZ YOURSELF:
The Bountiful Utah Temple is one of only two temples dedicated by President Howard W. Hunter during his brief time as President of the Church. What was the other?

BOUNTIFUL
Utah Temple

ANSWE
The Orlan
Florida Tem

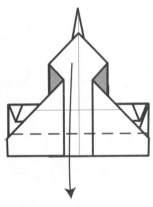

25. Fold top down.

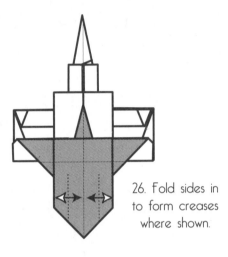

26. Fold sides in to form creases where shown.

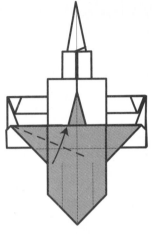

27. Fold where shown to form crease.

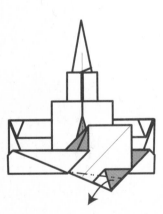

28. Fold top layer down using a swivel fold & squash the top layer flat (squash fold).

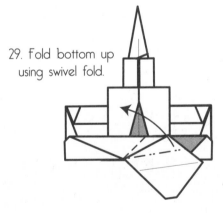

29. Fold bottom up using swivel fold.

30. Repeat steps 27-29 on the right side.

BOUNTIFUL
Utah Temple

DID YOU KNOW:
The Bountiful Temple is the eighth temple built in Utah & the first in Davis County.

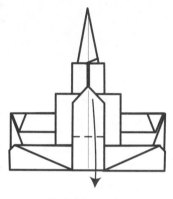

31. Fold top layer down where shown.

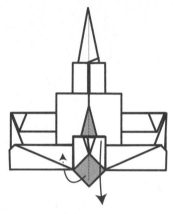

32. Unfold top layer & fold tab behind.

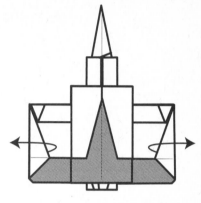

33. Unfold side tabs.

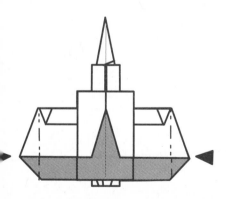

34. Open model slightly & push sides in (inside fold).

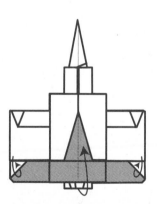

35. Fold bottom up & tuck corners into the pockets.

36. Finished!

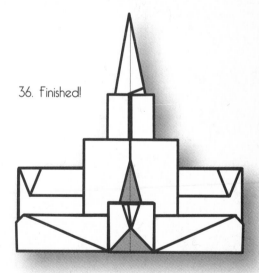

artwork: Nick Robinson
design: Andrew Hudson

DID YOU KNOW:
Announcement: 3 October 2009.
Groundbreaking Ceremony: Anticipated to occur in 2014.

CONCEPCIÓN
Chile Temple

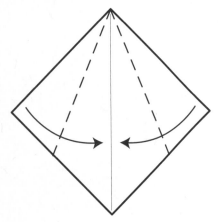

1. Start with a square piece of paper. Fold the side corners to the center.

2. Fold the sides & bottom to where the corners meet & unfold.

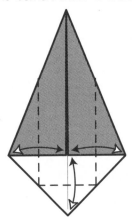

3. Fold where shown & unfold.

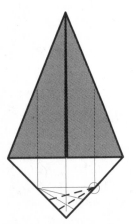

4. Fold where shown on other side & unfold. Turn paper over.

5. Pleat sides & unfold. Turn paper over.

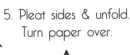

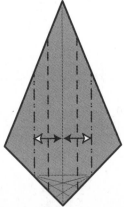

6. Fold bottom up.

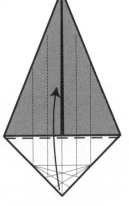

QUIZ YOURSELF:

he Concepción Chile Temple
ll be the second temple built
Chile. What was the first &
hen was it built?

CONCEPCIÓN
Chile Temple

ANSWER:

Santiago Chile Temple,
built in 1983.

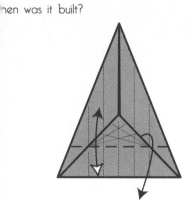

7. Fold bottom up &
unfold to step 6.

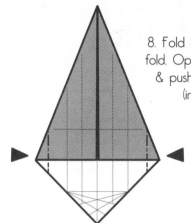

8. Fold corners in & un-
fold. Open model slightly
& push corners inside
(inside fold).

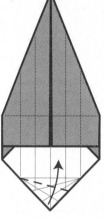

9. Using existing crease, fold
left side of bottom flap up.

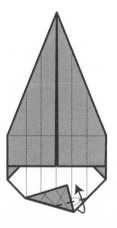

10. Using existing crease, fold
right side of bottom up.

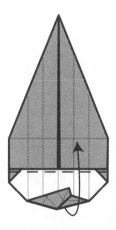

11. Fold bottom up.

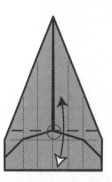

12. Fold bottom up at
point shown & unfold.

57

CONCEPCIÓN
Chile Temple

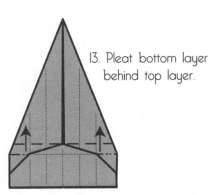

13. Pleat bottom layer behind top layer.

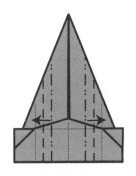

14. Pleat sides in where shown.

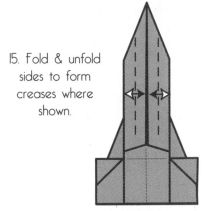

15. Fold & unfold sides to form creases where shown.

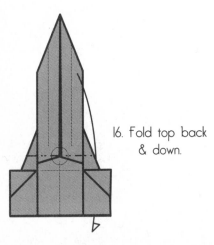

16. Fold top back & down.

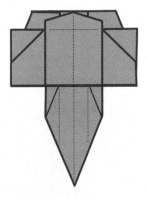

17. Turn paper over.

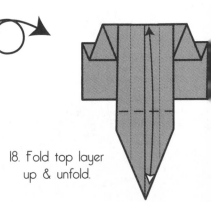

18. Fold top layer up & unfold.

58

CONCEPCIÓN
Chile Temple

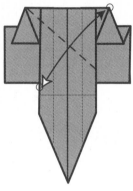

19. Fold & unfold to form crease where shown.

20. Repeat step 19 on opposite side.

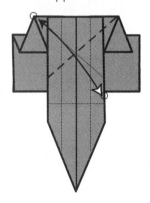

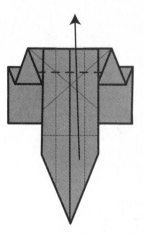

21. Fold top layer up.

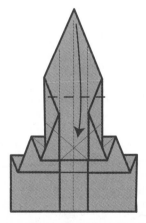

22. Fold down on existing crease.

23. Fold & unfold to form crease where shown.

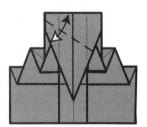

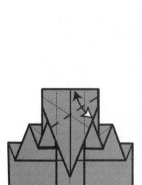

24. Repeat step 23 on opposite side but don't unfold.

59

CONCEPCIÓN

Chile Temple

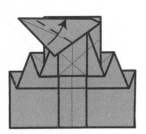

25. Fold along the crease from step 23.

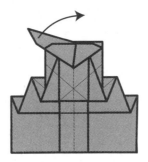

26. Fold spire up using a swivel fold.

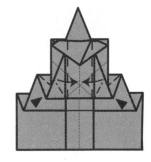

27. Fold sides in & squash flaps flat (squash fold).

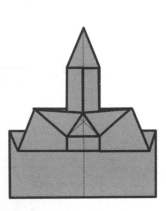

28. Turn paper over.

29. Finished!

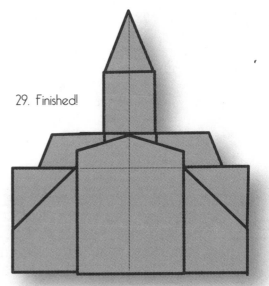

artwork: Nick Robin·
design: Andrew Hud·

ANCHORAGE
Alaska Temple

skill level: 2

DID YOU KNOW:
The Anchorage Alaska Temple was the first temple built in Alaska.

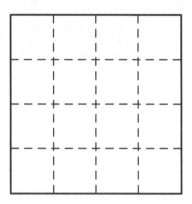

1. Start with a square piece of paper. Fold in half twice top to bottom & twice side to side & unfold so that the creases have formed 16 squares as shown.

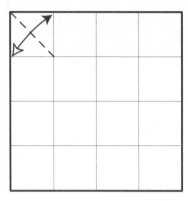

2. Fold & unfold the top left corner to establish crease.

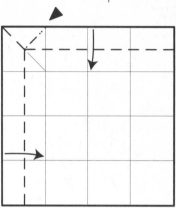

3. Make a rabbit-ear fold by folding the top down & left side in so that the resulting flap extends up.

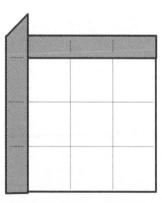

4. Turn paper over.

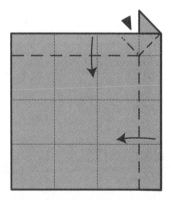

5. Rabbit-ear fold again by folding the top down & right side in so the tower extends up.

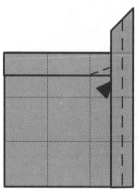

6. Fold right flap in half left to right & squash fold the layer underneath it.

ANCHORAGE
Alaska Temple

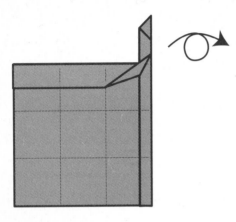

7. Turn paper over.

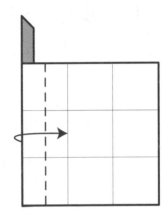

8. Fold left side over.

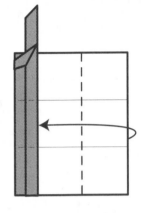

9. Fold right side over to the edge.

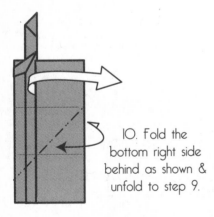

10. Fold the bottom right side behind as shown & unfold to step 9.

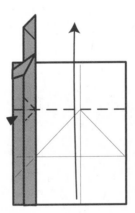

11. Fold the bottom up, unfolding the edge as you do so.

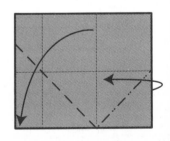

12. Fold right side down & squash flaps flat (squash fold).

ANCHORAGE
Alaska Temple

skill level: 2

DID YOU KNOW:
Announcement: 4 October 1997.
Groundbreaking & Site
Dedication: 17 April 1998 by F.
Melvin Hammond.
Dedication: 9-10 January 1999
by Gordon B. Hinckley.

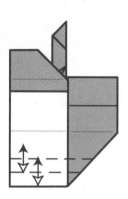

13. Fold & unfold bottom twice to establish two creases.

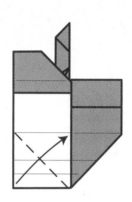

14. Fold bottom left corner up.

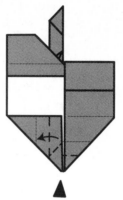

15. Fold bottom point up while folding flap to left (swivel fold).

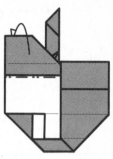

16. Carefully fold top flap behind.

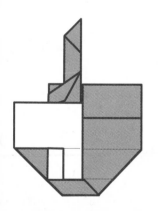

17. Turn paper over.

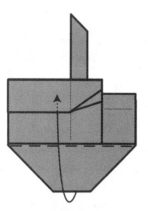

18. Fold bottom up & tuck inside.

19. Finished!

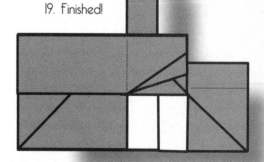

artwork: Nick Robinson
design: Andrew Hudson

NEWPORT
Beach California Temple

DID YOU KNOW:
Announcement: 21 April 2001.
Groundbreaking & Site Dedication:
15 August 2003 by Duane B.
Gerrard.
Dedication: 28 August 2005 by
Gordon B. Hinckley.

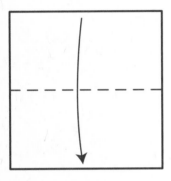

1. Start with a square piece of paper. Fold in half top to bottom.

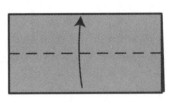

2. Fold top layer up.

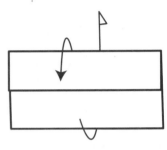

3. Unfold everything & turn over.

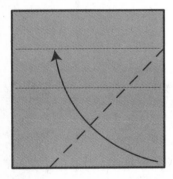

4. Fold bottom right corner up to top crease.

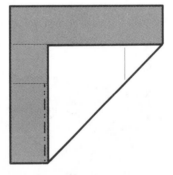

5. Crease where indicated. Turn paper over.

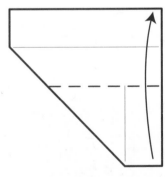

6. Fold bottom up.

NEWPORT
Beach California Temple

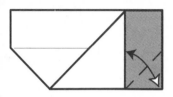

7. Fold lower right corner up.

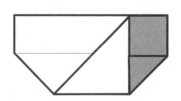

8. Unfold to step 6.

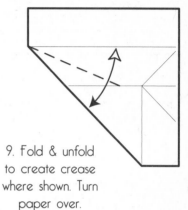

9. Fold & unfold to create crease where shown. Turn paper over.

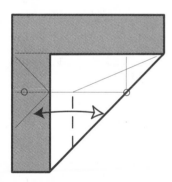

10. Fold & unfold right to left to create a crease that lines up with the end of the crease from step 9.

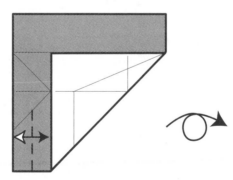

11. Fold & unfold bottom of left flap to create crease where shown. Turn paper over.

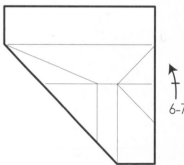

6-7

12. Repeat steps 6-7.

65

NEWPORT
Beach California Temple

DID YOU KNOW:
On January 13, 2005, during the placement of the statue of the angel Moroni, a remarkable solar halo was visible, which surrounded the sun. Once Moroni was in place, the phenomenon dissipated.

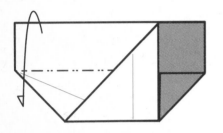

13. Fold bottom layer behind.

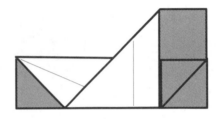

14. Turn paper over.

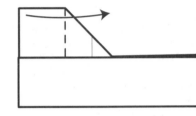

15. Fold left side of bottom layer over without unfolding the layers around it.

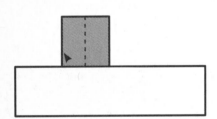

16. Fold right side of bottom layer over without unfolding the layers around it.

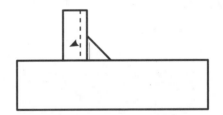

17. Fold small portion of right edge over (see step 18 for spacing).

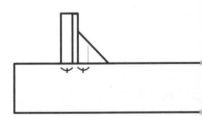

18. Model should have equal spacing at spots shown. Turn paper over.

NEWPORT
Beach California Temple

QUIZ YOURSELF:
What three changes did the Church make to the original design of the temple to satisfy the local community?

ANSWER:
Shortened the steeple. changed the color of the outside of the temple & agreed to turn off floodlights by ll pm every night.

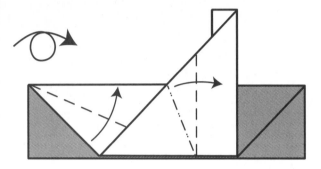

19. Fold top layer up & to the right using a swivel fold.

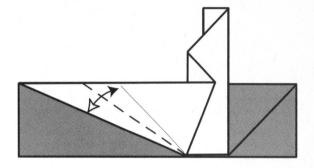

20. Fold & unfold top layer where shown.

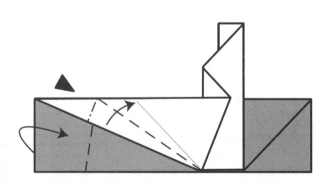

21. Fold left side over & use a squash fold to flatten flap.

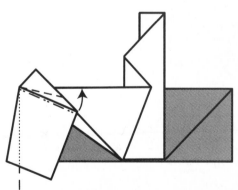

22. Fold upper layer up using a swivel fold so that the bottom edge lies on itself.

NEWPORT
Beach California Temple

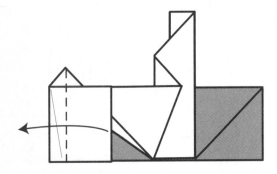

23. Fold top layer back out where shown.

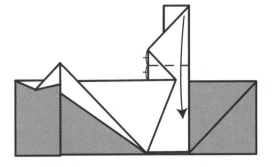

24. Fold the spire down matching the left corner to the edge of the roof.

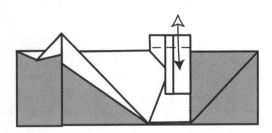

25. Fold & unfold the top flap where shown.

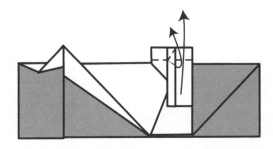

26. Fold top layer up using a swivel fold.

NEWPORT
Beach California Temple

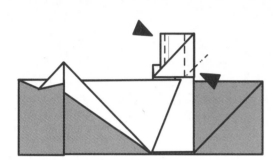

27. Fold sides in to thin the spire & flatten corners (squash fold).

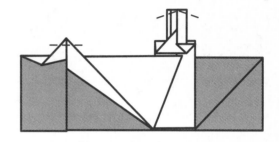

28. Fold down corners to round the spire & the dome.

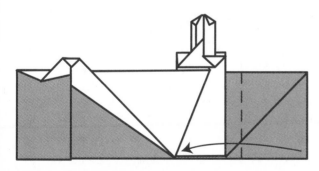

29. Fold right side to the left side of spire.

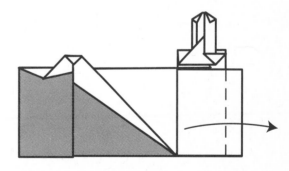

30. Fold flap back out along the right side of the spire.

69

NEWPORT
Beach California Temple

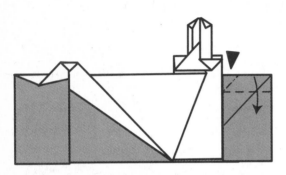

31. Fold top of right side down as far as squash fold will allow.

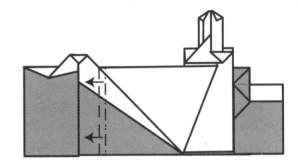

32. Make a small pleat to form the edge of the other tower.

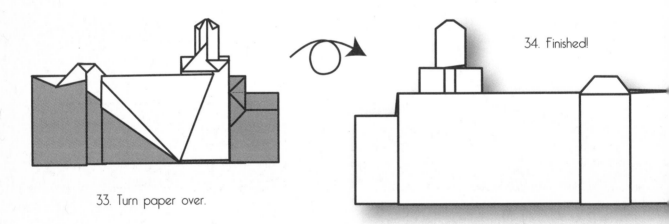

33. Turn paper over.

34. Finished!

artwork: Nick Robir
design: Andrew Hud

TOKYO
Japan Temple

DID YOU KNOW:
Announcement: 9 August 1975.
Construction Commencement:
10 April 1978.
Dedication: 27-29 October 1980
by Spencer W. Kimball.

1. Start with a square piece of paper. Pinch the midpoint where shown.

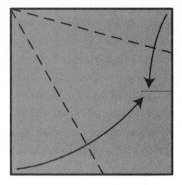

2. Fold the bottom left corner up & the top right corner down to the crease from step 1.

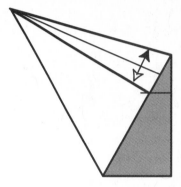

3. Fold the upper flap up.

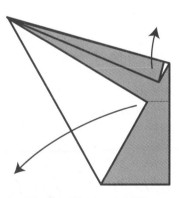

4. Unfold everything.

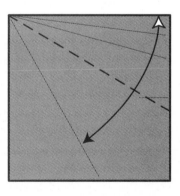

5. Fold & unfold top right corner down to crease from step 2.

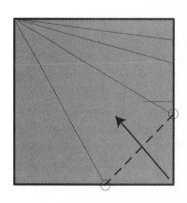

6. Fold bottom right corner up where shown.

71

TOKYO
Japan Temple

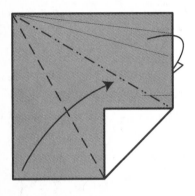

7. Fold bottom left corner up & top right corner behind.

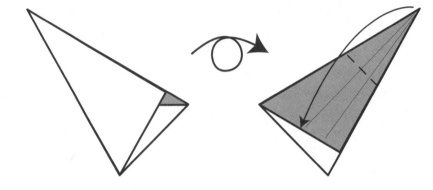

8. Turn paper over.

9. Fold point down to where shown.

10. Fold top left corner down & unfold.

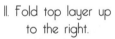

11. Fold top layer up to the right.

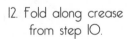

12. Fold along crease from step 10.

13. Swivel fold spire so it points up.

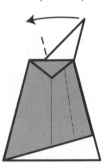

72

TOKYO
Japan Temple

14. Unfold to step 12.

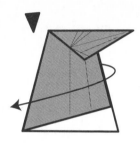

15. Pull out one layer & flatten it to the left.

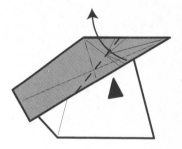

16. Fold flap up squashing the hidden edge (Squash fold).

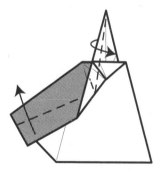

17. Fold edge up (swivel fold) using the crease from step 3.

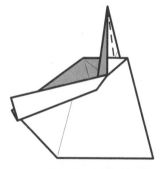

18. Fold the right side of steeple in to match. Turn paper over.

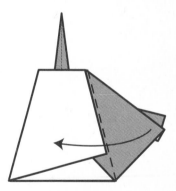

19. Fold right side back down.

TOKYO
Japan Temple

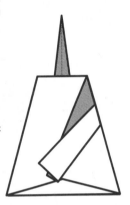

20. Reverse the order of the three layers.

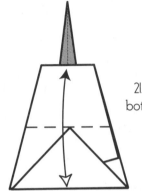

21. Fold in half bottom to top & unfold.

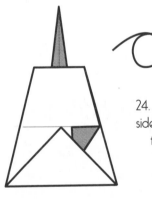

22. Fold & unfold the middle layer to create crease.

23. Turn paper over.

24. Fold & unfold sides in to create two creases.

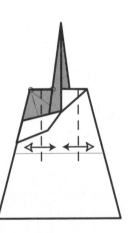

TOKYO
Japan Temple

QUIZ YOURSELF:
Which General Authority first prophecied regarding the Tokyo Japan Temple?

ANSWER:
On Sunday. July 17. 1949. Elder Matthew Cowley made the first prophecy regarding the Tokyo Japan Temple at the dedicatory services for the old Tokyo Mission Home—the site where the temple now stands.

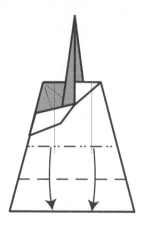

25. Pleat top down.

26. Fold sides in & squash folds flat (squash fold).

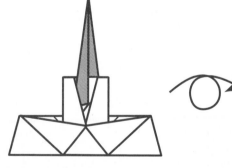

27. Turn paper over.

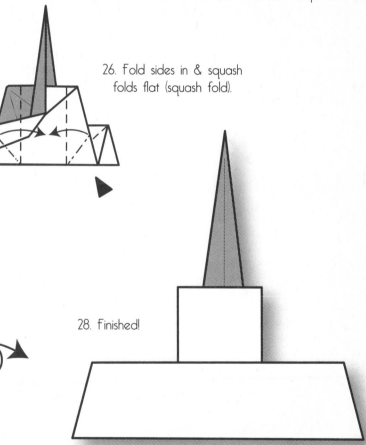

28. Finished!

artwork: Nick Robinson

design: Andrew Hudson

DID YOU KNOW:
Announcement: 13 February 1994.
Groundbreaking & Site Dedication:
13 May 1995 by Gordon B. Hinckley.
Dedication: 2-4 November 1997 by
Gordon B. Hinckley.

VERNAL
Utah Temple

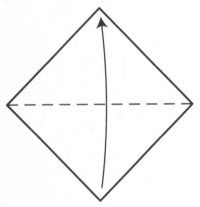

1. Start with a square piece of paper. Fold in half bottom to top.

2. Fold in half right to left & unfold.

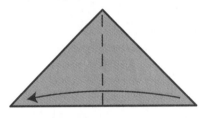

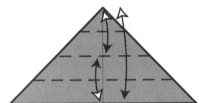

3. Fold in half bottom to top & unfold. Fold bottom & top to center crease to make four sections. Unfold everything.

5. Fold flap down just below crease line.

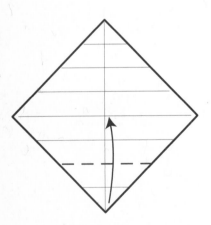

4. Fold bottom up where shown.

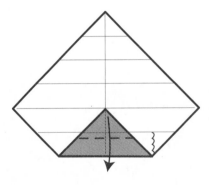

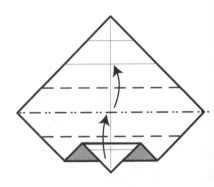

6. Pleat bottom up.

VERNAL
Utah Temple

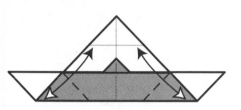

7. Fold & unfold
sides.

8. Open flaps & fold sides
up (inside fold).

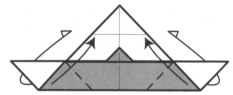

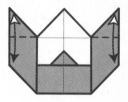

9. Fold side points
down & unfold.

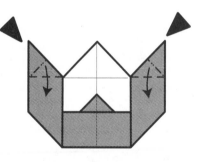

10. Push sides in & fold
flaps down (squash fold).

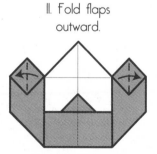

11. Fold flaps
outward.

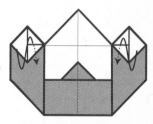

12. Fold flaps inside.

DID YOU KNOW:

The Vernal Utah Temple is labeled 1907 & 1997, indicating the two years when the building was dedicated—first as a tabernacle & then as a temple.

VERNAL
Utah Temple

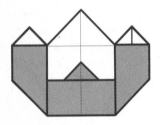

13. Turn paper over.

14. Pull out paper from left flap.

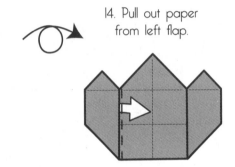

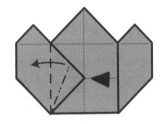

15. Fold flap to right & squash flap flat (squash fold).

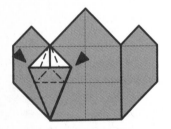

16. Push sides together & fold down (petal fold). Repeat steps 14-16 on right side.

17. Fold top down.

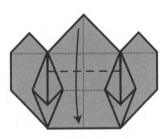

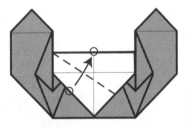

18. Fold flap up where shown.

VERNAL
Utah Temple

19. Fold where shown & unfold.
Unfold to step 18 & repeat steps
18-19 on opposite side.

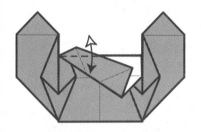

20. Fold & unfold at two
places shown.

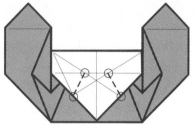

21. Fold flap up.

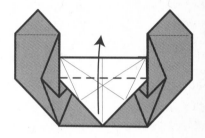

22. Fold sides of flap
toward the center &
flatten flaps (squash fold).

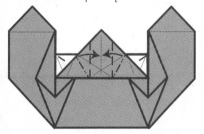

23. Fold flaps down.
Fold sides in.

24. Fold side spires
inward.

VERNAL
Utah Temple

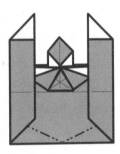

25. Tuck bottom corners inside to lock spires in place.

28. Finished!

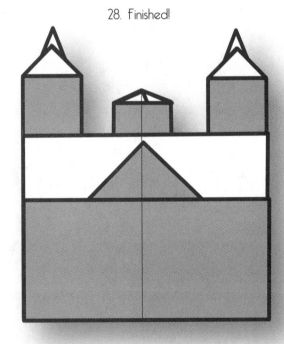

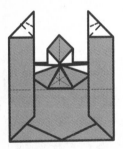

26. Pleat tips of spires so they point up. Turn paper over.

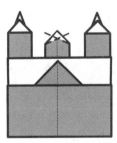

27. Fold down each side of center tower.

artwork: Nick Robins
design: Andrew Huds

WASHINGTON
DC Temple

DID YOU KNOW:
Announcement: 15 November 1968.
Groundbreaking & Site
Dedication: 7 December 1968 by
Hugh B. Brown.
Dedication: 19-22 November 1974
by Spencer W. Kimball.

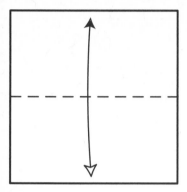

1. Start with a square piece of paper. Fold in half top to bottom & unfold.

2. Fold bottom right corner up where shown & unfold.

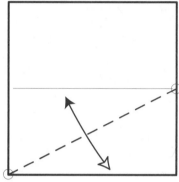

3. Fold in half top right corner to bottom left corner & unfold.

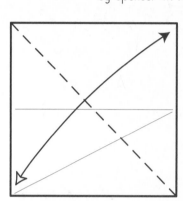

4. At intersection of creases from steps 2 & 3, fold & unfold bottom up & right side to left.

5. Fold & unfold left side & top to lines from step 4.

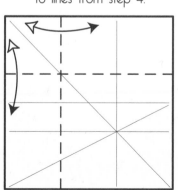

6. Fold in half bottom to top.

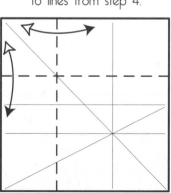

81

WASHINGTON
DC Temple

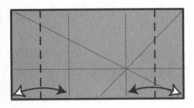

7. Fold left & right sides in & unfold.

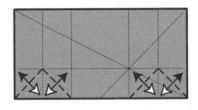

8. Fold & unfold to establish four small creases where shown.

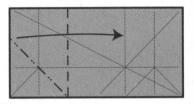

9. Fold top layer of left side over & flatten flap (squash fold).

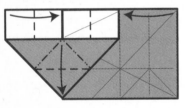

10. Pull top layer down & fold sides in (petal fold).

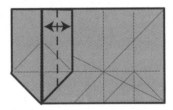

11. Fold & unfold left flap where shown. Repeat steps 9-11 on opposite side.

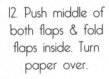

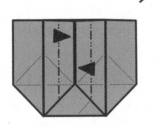

12. Push middle of both flaps & fold flaps inside. Turn paper over.

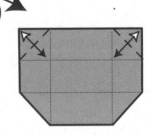

13. Fold & unfold top corners.

WASHINGTON
DC Temple

skill level: 3

DID YOU KNOW:
The Washington DC Temple
is the tallest temple in the
Church at a height
of 288 feet.

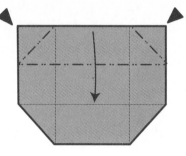

14. Pull top down & fold
sides in (squash fold).

15. Push four corners inside
(inside fold).

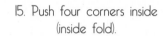

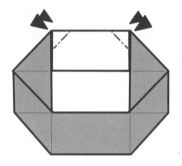

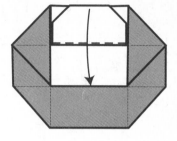

16. Pull down the top layer to
open the pleats on each side.

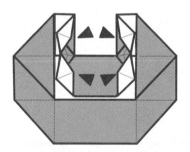

17. Push from the inside to
flatten everything.

18. Fold & unfold
sides.

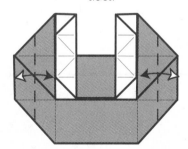

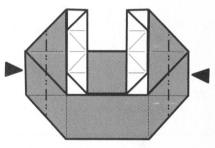

19. Push sides in & tuck
inside (inside fold).

WASHINGTON
DC Temple

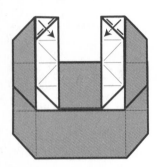

20. Tuck two corners underneath where shown.

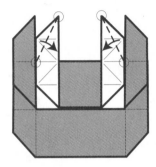

21. Fold middle towers to thin spires.

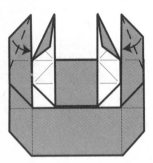

22. Fold outer towers to thin spires.

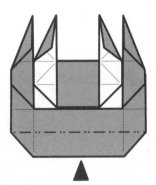

23. Push bottom up & tuck inside.

WASHINGTON
DC Temple

skill level: 3

DID YOU KNOW:
The Washington DC Temple has seven floors, which represent the six days of creation & the day of rest.

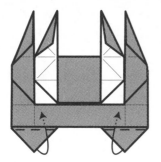

24. Fold flaps into pocket to lock the model.

26. Finished!

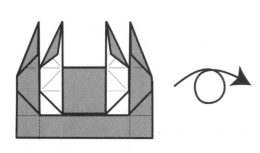

25. Turn paper over.

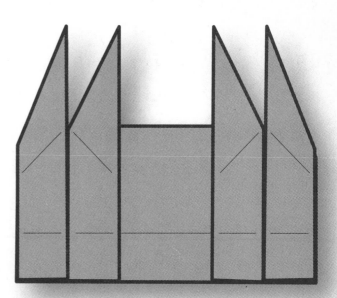

artwork: Nick Robinson

design: Andrew Hudson

INDEX

BY SKILL LEVEL

ABOUT THE AUTHOR

Todd Huisken is a licensed marriage and family therapist practicing in Irvine, California. He attended Brigham Young University and the University of San Diego and has a master's degree in Marriage and Family Therapy. His love for creative teaching methods began when he served as an early morning seminary teacher for six years. He is the author of *The Dating Directory* and *Mormon Origami*. The most important thing about Todd is that he has been married to his beautiful wife for twenty-four years, and they have three daughters and a son. They try to make Disneyland their second home.